BIRD~BRAIN

Also by Matt Mauch

If You're Lucky Is a Theory of Mine
Trio House Press

Prayer Book

Bird~Brain

Poems by Matt Mauch

Copyright © Matt Mauch 2017

No part of this book may be used or performed without written consent from the author, if living, except for critical articles or reviews.

Mauch, Matt
1st edition.

ISBN: 978-0-9965864-4-3
Library of Congress Control Number: 2016908750

Interior Layout by Lea C. Deschenes
Cover Design by Dorinda Wegener
Cover Art by Sara Lefsyk
Editing by Tayve Neese and Sara Lefsyk

Printed in Tennessee, USA
Trio House Press, Inc.
Ponte Vedra Beach, FL

To contact the author, send an email to tayveneese@comcast.net.

For Mike Wilson.
Outliving you reshapes what living means and is.
Goodbye again.

Table of Contents

I

For every obvious thing, there's a three-dimensional chess set of subtextual things	3
What you won't see here is Orion, for it's neither winter nor night (a Uruguayan, you couldn't see the Southern Cross)	6
She loves me, she loves me not	8
People being mostly water and not nocturnal	10
Holding a paper bag full of true truths, folded over at the top, no streamers, fireworks, or confetti geysering out	11
You say, "Promise"	13
The true story of how I learned that the graveyard shift meets at Prince's for drinks at 6:30 a.m.	14
The clog I can't get unclogged, which I'll probably never tell you about (the drinking on company time that I will)	16
This is the brain stuck on a line from a movie	18

Poem like an old thumb-on-the-spool baitcasting reel,
meant to be attached to a rod to practice with in the park,
rather than hang useless on nails in your garage,
so that if or when you get a magic lamp the practice
pays off, and what you don't do is freeze, losing
your one shot with a genie emerged   20

A new day is what it was in a way that every day isn't   22

"May you live through a thousand winters," like "aloha,"
is our greeting   23

Kneeling before a casket   25

Grease-monkey aria   26

Thoughts like the molecules of exhaust that graduate
to visibility as they exit a tailpipe, tho' never last long
enough to shape themselves into rhinos or yachts or
friendly ghosts (as clouds do), serving only to remind
you it's cold   28

When will it be too late to apply lessons learned?   29

Like a matryoshka doll separated from the set
during some long-ago settling of affairs   31

May they all, your dreams, come true in the end   32

In order that I shall last as long as I can   35

II

Poem like the brain and a bright day conspiring to
wake me early to introduce me to a power I'll need
time to experiment with in order to understand all
I'm capable of   39

Another attempt at a sun ode   41

When you called to talk on New Year's Day   44

In this adventure of the rains, the runoff,   46

The other magicians will kill me for revealing all this 48

Allegory of the beached   50

A winter wind storm lead-pipes and cheap shots the
wind chime, like wind isn't a thing but things acting
in the fashion of a mob,   52

A cold spell like this can keep you in the house
all gathered up like an oligarch   54

I can see the heart of the city now that the trees are nude 56

And you thought I was dancing   57

The brain before it's donated to science   60

"it's not your normal eclipse," says
one blinded by it   62

III

Poem presented as an excuse for being so late	67
It's October, and a lot of things, including the usual carpetbaggers, summer, and the leaves on trees, are gone or going	69
I forgot my umbrella and am starting to see things newly now, as if with seldom-used eyes at the back of my head	71
You can't take it back after you click SEND	72
The brain in the body in the house whose owner you curse, call a lazy piece of shit	74
Old me would go from holding-up to leading, would put the transmission into gear and drive	76
Poem like the stock in which the Thanksgiving turkey lasts all winter, assuaging in a way that time never will by pretending to make time stand still	78
A public slide where the gleaming steel has been shinned just about frictionless by asses in blue jeans and also in fancier clothes	80
Another attempt at an ode to the cardinal	82
There's soup in the dome of my ladle too deep to lick out, my tongue not the tongue of an anteater,	83
This is the brain wishing Dr. Frankenstein had perfected his procedure, that one of his protégé could transplant it into a body made of younger parts	85

Where I-494 delineates suburban Bloomington from suburban Richfield	88
The serendipity of good light for taking photos in	90
Half of the battle of learning is learning what it is you can write for yourself	93
If you hit your man harder than he hits he you, he's the one who'll hurt more works for football, not for collisions with the sun	95
The question the Farmer's Almanac answers about winter is whether it will be mild or harsh, but the question I have isn't that	97
Ruminations on the cud from seven of my fullest stomachs	98
It's on the way back that walking there starts to seem like a bad idea	101
There but for	103
In addition to watching a football game none of our teams are playing in	105
This is the brain feeling slighted, and so adopting mechanisms pursuant to its defense	107
Stretching for a run to work off more than just the take-out you've been eating so much of,	109
Acknowledgments	113

In India there is a bird called a semenda *whose beak has several distinct pipes with many openings. When death approaches, the bird collects a quantity of dry wood in its nest, and sitting upon it, sings so sweetly with all its pipes that it attracts and soothes all listeners to a marvelous degree. Then, igniting the wood by flapping its wings, it allows itself to be burnt to death.*

– Eliot Weinberger

I said: what we've lost is a story
and what we've never had
a song.

– Robert Hass

I

For every obvious thing, there's a three-dimensional chess set of subtextual things

that a songbird, arrived from summering north of here,
reminds me of, of

all that I've lost. The bird, like an estate sale ad
packed with so many implausibly well-kept

treasures, it's no big thing it has a heart,
can fly away when it needs to,

sings as if it's been sinkhole-swallowing
fairy-tale endings

since the dawn of story time, is blowing them stunningly
out now along the trough of a rolled wet tongue

aimed at the window I once took a photograph of lightning through.

To stop on a chain-link fence
rather than down by the lake

or among the leaves, dew-laundered
and drying out in the trees,

means the bird must be burdened by things

things with wings are seldom burdened by, most flyers
not from here content to fly on, though what beyond flying

farther south this one must augur
or prophesy or presage

(or change if it arrived
in a time machine), who can say

before the inciting act? Pistol that's not a pistol
not yet hung on the wall,

the point-of-view character who'll tell our stories hence
still conducting research

with binoculars,
hoping to get one of us in bed, pin us against a wall,

bend us over a chair or corner us in a stopped elevator
before the credits roll. Everybody

we can think of who got us here
listed (alphabetically or in order of appearance),

names going by so fast
nobody's able to read them. The garages

all along the alley enough like a canyonned city, Tuesday

enough like rehearsal space,
morning enough like an opening scene,

that the bird making a ruckus
and I are, as we all are at all beginnings: anonymous,

in windows in skyscrapers
yet to be zoomed in on,

making up aubades.

In the pre-dawn dark, in the post-dawn light,
somebody says our name, and it sounds like

our name with a decodable message
hidden in it, as with invisible ink, and the message

could be, *I can clean/tap dance/sew*
if you can cook/remember birthdays/tell jokes well/mow,

or it could be any number of things,
which is why we turn,

hoping what we heard is
exactly what we thought we did.

What you won't see here is Orion, for it's neither winter nor night (a Uruguayan, you couldn't see the Southern Cross)

A phenomenon one can shake off
like a fly on the hand

if considered in terms of its thermodynamics, but if considered
in terms of an animal nature

being present in one, not the other,

the fact that the temperature of the air above the asphalt
is palpably warmer than the temperature of the air

above the grass,
if you feel it with your vulnerable parts,

feels like the asphalt exhaling,
and can lead one to scratch one's calf

absentmindedly, and in my case led to dragging
a fingernail across a burn still healing.

It was as if I were a snake
with a one-lunged, transparent-eyelided way of seeing things.

As if I were in the asphalt's mouth.

The me that was didn't slither but walked to the middle of a bridge
where the shadows of the trees and the shadow of me

were like giants who couldn't shake hands.

I kept trying. You could see my shadow leaning, reaching
out to the left, the right.

Though reacher, I had the smallest shadow.
The bridge was over a river, not a road.

The water was as black as night in the country
and got blacker the more that I stared.

It took staring to see
that the river had what rivers don't call a heart. It took

staring even longer
to see that it had, perhaps, two or three hundred
                              of them.

That it was agile enough to swallow things you wouldn't have bet it could
didn't stop me from making the constellation

man with more arms and legs than most,
reaching both out and down.

I was thinking like a net when I thought,
I can save you from your death

if you're falling here and now.

There wasn't a tone, but there was something like it,
telling me to turn the page.

She loves me, she loves me not

My hand, like a squirrel
with ambitions beyond its ken,

moves the papers on a desk, finds and picks up a pen.

The brain has bypassed the lips,
is instructing the fingers to write, *I say*.

(Through them it says, s*ay goodbye
to half a minute you'll never see again.*)

Had the lips intercepted the signal,
I would have told you sincerely by now,

good morning. I would have said, *it looks warm out, the sun's out,
I think maybe I'll clean the gutters*, maybe sit at a corner table

over a bowl of chili, a waiter or waitress
bringing beers, where the hand, the fingers

will say that one of the principle differences
between a daisy and the moon

is that the daisy knows what to do when
the sun says, *Come hither.*

The hand adds *nonpareil* to a list of words it should use
in a sentence. It writes,

swear by the daisy, even if she loves you not.

A leaf (a little raking
is what I've done next)

wears its red dress, parties
for three or four or five straight days and nights

before it burns out, becomes a gutter leaf, or bag leaf,
is what the hand with the pen in it writes

before the brain makes it say that *even the voluptuous lips*
of a moon crater

eventually erode into so much dust
in the light moon wind. The brain and hand

in concert write that *the lips of a daisy open once,*
like a booster stage in a moon shot

sending a flower into orbit,

and a tenuous equilibrium orbit is, a kind of house arrest
you never want to end,

where the oar-shaped petals of re-entry,
with their knowledge of the times ahead,

wait to be plucked and put into service,
all for one, one for all.

**People being mostly water
and not nocturnal**

What I aspire to is the example of the day moon,
seeing and being seen,

emeritus, laying my moon hands,
which are as immune from prosecution

as a diplomat's hands,

on your stomach, forehead, cheek, nape,
all around both of your thighs, playing

tic-tac-toe,
or Scrabble, or cribbage,

shaking out my moon dice

on your nakedness, in game after game
with all of your tides.

**Holding a paper bag full of true truths, folded over at the top,
no streamers, fireworks, or confetti geysering out**

No announcement (who to, who from),
these true truths staining the bag

like buttered popcorn. You

naming the shapes—
nipple afloat, disembodied wing, hippopotamus drinking gin—

overcoming the fear that a jealous Athena
may turn you into the paper bag itself. You stand

in front of the projector, good practice
for when you'll stand

in front of some sun, blocking this view as that,
the shadow of you on the screen

throwing *eyeball steeping in traffic, balsa-wood heart,
ambition as clouds at rest*

at enemies, friends, frenemies,
exes, crushes, unrequited loves. They

turn and mutter breathy *god-damns*
and *Jesus Christs*,

shielding their faces from the light

with body parts
they thought were impenetrable, but now must wield

as things permeable
and glowing.

You say, "Promise"

You mean,
like an arrow nocked and a bow drawn. I hear,

like the recently hatched, featherless
and blind

among brothers and sisters
just as featherless, just as blind

all shivering.

**The true story of how I learned that the graveyard shift
meets at Prince's for drinks at 6:30 a.m.**

A real-life bird that didn't stay long
in its spotlight of sun,

not long enough for me to figure out
whether its feathers were black or a blue so dark

I can call it black and get away with it.
Blue or black or blue-black bird

inspiring the mind-made bird
I call idea of bird

that starred in my dream last night.
Shortly after the dream began, idea of bird

shat on an ex boss of mine to earn my trust.
The dream was like the two-hour pilot in a series, the promise

of revelations in additional episodes
making it okay that real bird

was fleeting. Idea of bird
is what I'm shadow to. Flying, (a), but also flying,

(b), sans harness next to the bird
with its grape-sized clone of Upton Sinclair's heart

is what I think of when I'm not with the bird
and anybody says,

eternal flame. Once we figured out we're not substantial
enough to be picked up on radar, it gave

idea of bird and I a sort of carte blanche:
we opened up the phone lines to requests from the masses.

I wake in the mornings, now,
exhausted after nights of me aiming and idea of bird dropping

our messily retributive bombs. Because I never wear
my Che Guevara t-shirts

anymore, there's little that the authorities can do
to finger me. Idea of bird and I have this running joke

about Santa Claus, *and what a fucking claus he is*, we say,
working one night out of 365.

We say it loud enough to be overheard. Those who don't laugh,
we tell ourselves, in a second over-hear-able aside, like

we're whistleblowers
leaking what everybody for their own good ought to know,

either are human and can't be trusted
or are a North Pole strain of elf, and so not even real at all.

**The clog I can't get unclogged,
which I'll probably never tell you about
(the drinking on company time that I will)**

I raise the plunger
like an ax.

I see a face
rising from the imperfections
in the porcelain, from the chips
and stains.

I try to swing
hard but it feels like I'm swinging
in slow motion, as if I'm inside of
amber.

I see a second face
and a third, and each has earned
its measure of blame.

I feel a me given up for dead
bullying its way through the ruins
of my shoulders, my back.

I *whack* and *whack*
and *whack* and *whack* and *whack*
and *whack*

wildly at the clog, at the sink,
at the whole expanse
of sewer and city
and job.

                    Through a cubicle wall
                    I wish were porous,

        pictures we wish were portals to where we'd rather be
                            tacked to either side (kin

        of the transparencies we use to vote against shitty views),

                                    you ask me what
                                    I had for lunch and
                                    how was it, and

                                    because your words,
                                    after I wait a bit,
                        don't cool or condense into better song,

                I tell you, *Tecates two for one*
        to go with chile verde and eggs over easy on the side (the eggs

            an extra dollar twenty-five, the hens that laid them,
                    if realized, are realized by what we do
                            while they're inside us).

This is the brain stuck on a line from a movie

Like the unbreakable that breaks, the unsinkable that sinks,
the beautiful brain dithers, doesn't invent a thing,

won't synthesize "soar" with "crash," just says,
Every time a bell rings

an angel gets his wings, repeats it
like an LP with an imperfection
in a groove intended to be smooth,

like a highway in need of repair
in a brain that holds a universe of roads we

forget the lines we were memorizing
when we find a twenty on the sidewalk,

when, because of nice weather and an open window,
a parakeet riffs off of a cardinal on a wire.

The parakeet is in a cage. The cage is in a house.
The cardinal is channeling sounds trapped in the wire.

The intercepting brain sends flowers to our ears.
(It would invent the telegraph, or wireless communication,

or the lyrics to "We Shall Overcome,"
if we didn't already have them.) The brain wants to show
both the parakeet and the cardinal

a world without them: hecklers at chamber performances,
loud talkers at the cinema,

chirpers chirping in November
same as they chirped in June (like

earnest vote after earnest vote
against one's own

socio-economic interests). The brain makes the hand reach
into the pocket that isn't there

to pull out neither the petals of a rose, nor a rabbit from a hat,

but silence, which it brings to the on-looking
and thus far overlooked sparrow, silence

being the world without it, which for the sparrow is despair,
and in the daydream this all happens while it's snowing,

and after despair witnessed by the empathetic
but not currently despairing,

each snowflake is the soul of a sparrow, or can be.

**Poem like an old thumb-on-the-spool baitcasting reel,
meant to be attached to a rod to practice with in the park,
rather than hang useless on nails in your garage,
so that if or when you get a magic lamp the practice
pays off, and what you don't do is freeze, losing
your one shot with a genie emerged**

The first wish I wish you'd wish is that everybody's
windows worked as well as the mechanicals
say they should, the tight seal
the pencil, ruler, and compass make on the page
becoming the tight seal in the double-hung or casement
when a west wind blows. It's a wish
that grew from egg to tadpole in the brackish estuary
of self-preoccupation, because today, windows be damned,
the wind infiltrates. The snow isn't here to be beautiful.
It's utilitarian, like dye in a vein, recording
all these infiltrations, all the implicit exiting,
the wishes on behalf of humanity—big ones,
the intricacies of which would require lifetimes
of small-step wishes. So the wish I wish
you'd wish next, because we don't have lifetimes left,
is that a displaced and largely misunderstood
family of the lights having been attracted to the darks—
so now they're crossbred, these elves who I wish
you'd wish would move into your attic.
That they thank you for the roof and
Laissez-faire economics, eavesdropping on your dreams
for a better Bangladesh, a richer Haiti,
using their magic as a kind of rental payment
to make your dreams come true in your dreams at least.
And the third wish I wish you'd wish, for those
who've moved too many times, in vans and pickups,
on camels and in cars, on foot, packing and deciding
what to keep, what to leave behind—this third and last

wish being that they will own, settle, stay, remodel, redecorate.
That by never moving again they will find the time to boil
grits for those who love grits, the time to cook
food that the eaters crave. Each *thank you*,
belch, nap, or loosening of the belt is quid pro quo.
Within that last wish is the corollary wish
that can't be separated from the main wish
without killing them both, that you and I
will be invited over to eat. And so will the elves.
And after we eat, the elves will lead out a chain gain
of politicians, bankers, CEOs, and lobbyists.
And we'll watch them clean up, like they're evil
stepsisters, like we're Cinderella's revenge.
Sipping our amaretto, our port, whatever else the elves looted
when they made the politicians, bankers, CEOs,
and lobbyists slaves. So it's good I didn't promise you,
as I promised myself, that I wouldn't be
like this today. Good that the hours ahead are opaque.
That we can rub. That there may be something inside them.

A new day is what it was in a way that every day isn't

The snow melted inside and out.
We were beginning to stumble over the corpses winter leaves behind.
We lifted shades, opened windows, waited for the light to pasteurize.

The stacks of plans on end tables, desks, sills
(that were able to) rose and crashed like birds in a hurry to migrate.

We put a hundred old scenes into boxes
and escorted them off the premises.

The story behind the story of what we had been that season
was unabridged and free.

It was the day before trash day.
Our offering on the curb was like a glass of scotch on the house
poured from a bottle with a twist-off cap,

a life that had been lived and picked through,

the finds and steals already stolen and found
by those who came early and knew what to look for.

It reminded me of a FREE ALL DAY day
at a second-tier amusement park

as all you do for your summer vacation.

It was a Saturday. It felt like spring.
It was a Thursday. We both called in sick.

**"May you live through a thousand winters," like "aloha,"
is our greeting**

It's the old story—
the bird with wintertime reservations
in the Yucatan's

and mine: sojourner meets the hunker-down (bi-annually)
to share opposite truths

on how to make it through the coldest days
trusting the most resonant voices within.

I tell the bird, *Crawl when you need to.*
Protect your underside.

Use your wing like I use my hand, as a shield of last resort.
The bird tells me, *Your stomach, more so than your brain,*

is the part of you that remembers best
what needs remembering most.

I write down what the bird says on an index card
I carry in my pocket

on the opposite side of which
I write that I was born blue, drowning
in my mother's fluids.

The porcupine, opossum, and artichoke
protect the self with what the self provides,

thinking small, then smaller than that,
then smaller still,

till they become the issuers of the voices within.

The dormant and hibernating trees, grass, frogs, turtles, and bears
dream that they're inside the house

with all the lights on,

are at the party mingling.
Pretty soon it's spring. So, pretty soon they are.

"May both *live* and *winters* be broadly defined,"
is how we always say goodbye.

Kneeling before a casket

I crawl out of my skin, a la snake,

see my old hollow face

with a new wet one.

I vomit up a brook, cough out birds.

You probably didn't see.

Grease-monkey aria

I vacuum beneath and in the crotch of your seats,
and after cleaning the windows with ammonia-based spray,

inspect for smudges, breathe from the depths of me
on any I find, rub them away with my sleeve

like I'm a eulogy
taking the edge off of a complicated life.

Do you ever notice how legibly I try to warn you,
pressing as though I were a layer of heavy clay

through the carbon and three copies of the ticket?

When you arrive tall, I orchestrate the pedals with my toes,
making the first movement of your oil change
        a ballet.

When you're shorter than me, I drive into and out of the stall,
knees against the dash, as if your car were
                a womb.

In the twenty-four photos that will survive the mass extinction of me
(all the album holds),

are none of the derogatory names I've been called.

When all is well, I pine for you
the way a nation of unbuilt ramps

pined for wheelchairs
in the days before the Americans with Disabilities Act.

Do you think of me as one who flies on leathery old wings
in an age of feathers?

I, who am where you have been. I, to whom you are going.

Payer of homage to the length of your legs
no matter their length that day.

Thoughts like the molecules of exhaust that graduate to visibility as they exit a tailpipe, tho' never last long enough to shape themselves into rhinos or yachts or friendly ghosts (as clouds do), serving only to remind you it's cold

Driving through a town named after a lake larger than it is, where the speed limit drops to 45 (law demanding you savor the view), I watch a fisherman auger the ice, feel like a particle of air heated by the breath he blows into his palm, a novice being told by the master, *Seek refuge in the shadow of the lake's ceiling, in what lies beneath*, a point of view shared

with seaweed.

A girl on the ice etches the gray-blue lid with figure skates bought a half size too large to accommodate the extra wool of winter socks.

The overlay of figure eight upon figure eight tells me it's wise to forgive the transgressor
prior to the forgivable offense.

The town's like a moon caught in the gravitational pull of the lake.

I drive with one hand, write with the other on the back of a receipt for gas, "Whitecaps here are called *wild tears blooming*. There isn't a spring or fall, only *the short times when the winds and waters procreate*. The vernacular for water freezing over:

becomes an opal field that it takes all winter to sow and reap."

When will it be too late to apply lessons learned?

If I don't see soon
what's been hidden in murk

by the planet's great hiders of things, only gulls (et cetera)
will be able to keep up the search

or find a foundation or solace or respite
on what the lake will be become. The ice

I'm on is so thin an hour of 40 degrees will melt it.
I'll be like a bullet

shot through the window I've been peering into,
slowed down so you can see

me frame by frame.

I'm not the tie around anybody's neck.
I'm no one's pantyhose, not their dress shoes.

None have ever dropped me off at the dry cleaners, nor forced me to sit
in the ironing board's pew listening
to the steam's sermon.

I wouldn't mind being a belt as it's pulled through loops
as long as the person whose pants I'm cinching's got a tattoo that says,
Always wear a belt, even with your jeans.

All that I've found so far, all
that I've seen,
I've hidden like a sunken ship's cache

in a series of caves
that remind me of a hive
made out of an anatomically correct heart.

You won't be able to locate it (what I'm hoarding)
with your phone, nor even on a very old map.

All of this is a clue.

**Like a matryoshka doll separated from the set
during some long-ago settling of affairs**

I'm up before the sun can burn off the fog.
I stand at a plate-glass window

like a live model stands for a figure-drawing class,
holding a pose so it can be captured

inexpertly. I ogle the ghost of myself reflected in the fog-backed glass.
The ghost of myself ogles me.

The fog is like a sea of potato paste. In the distance
I see the masts of sailing ships. Soon enough the sun will reveal

the masts aren't masts but steeples.

The window I look out of is high in a house
on one side of a valley.

I wave a very tired arm,
wait for my wave to be received, translated, acknowledged.

I am naïve only if you refuse my membership
in a tribe that pipes radio transmissions

into space, builds parabolic dishes
deeper than lakes, listens

as its own kind starve.

May they all, your dreams, come true in the end

In the *I'm sure of it* footnote
to the "helicopter" entry

in the encyclopedia of inspiration
I'm drafting

(this meat of a tomato and its juices and skin
are the colors of sky

morning), it says

that the inventor of the helicopter, as a child,
studied the blade-like seeds of a maple tree.

He loved their rational, controlled, yet rapid descent.
His father told him to pluck the seeds that rooted and grew.

That was his job all June. Each time he plucked a seed
he wished he could teach next year's batch

(of which he presumed the tree was already dreaming)
an up to balance their dramatic downs.

He wanted the seeds to be able to repeat the trick.

The boy also dreamed he could kill his father and others
simply by wishing them,

accidentally, dead.

He didn't like that dream, the power he had in it,
but it kept recurring.

After the dull work of observing skiers and lifts,
he dreamed the helicopter, how it would be used in war.

He dreamed of a way to wage war
based on the rituals of the homecoming dance

and prom. He dreamed
he made the body-bag industry collapse.

The boy's dreams were the same dreams an ostrich dreamed.
The ostrich wrote its dreams down

in the dirt, hoping its progeny would invent a machine

that makes rotary-wing propulsion, and vertical takeoff,
and hovering obsolete.

The crows assigned to observe and record the ostrich and boy
had distinct vocal signatures

traceable to the regions where they were reared.

One reported what it observed with a call
that in English begins with a C.

Other dreams were reported in calls that began with a K.

Each call ended with a W sound, which is the English letter
(it must be)

that holds the institutional memory of crow.

The tomato sun, having completed its unhurried transmogrification
into less ambiguous light,

is now an onion sun. An involuntary shiver

makes me thankful for, and mindful of, the sense-making,
sense-harvesting qualities

of the cold. I put on

layers, walk the runway-like transitional space
(my silly draft done) between

the mountains and the river,

the river and the river, the stream and the creek,
the forest where it's thick

and the forest where it's thin, like a volunteer

maintaining safe passage
for snow-blindness,

for awe, under the jet stream of crows
telling me (tell me, crows,

all that you know).

In order that I shall last as long as I can

I, boiler of beans, shiner of shoes, sitter in chairs,

because I lived one sort of life
before I knew the secret to sawing a woman in half

and a different life after, refuse

to read anything about running
prior to running

lest the miracle of running (if there is one) diminish.

That's what happened yesterday
when I read about a double-blind study

to test for agents smaller than pheromones.
It was progress in the science of love,

an advancement I can't get out of my head,
can't stop thinking about,

and thinking about anything intently,
but perhaps, especially,

less mysterious love
while running

leads to tripping,
having to hold out hands as I'm baptized by ground.

If bloody (because of love) I knock on your door
seeking bandages and antiseptic,

I hope you have neither.
What I want you to offer

instead is some water and a vase
in which I can be pretty for a while

before I die.

II

**Poem like the brain and a bright day conspiring to wake me early
to introduce me to a power I'll need time to experiment with
in order to understand all I'm capable of**

A new sense, is what it is,
that stops me from stepping on the brown cat's tail

as the brown cat lies on the brown concrete
in the strangely browning light.

I've named the new sense Lucy (Antoinette
was runner-up).

Lucy suggests a reconsideration
of even the simplest of received truths,

and before I can say

why? says, *we call a robin's breast red
when it isn't.* Lucy makes me think

in the form of a garden slug
about what I've done/ not done, would/ wouldn't be willing to do.

I look up and around, like I'm not slug but snail, as if,

like the Rockefellers, I were born with a protective shell.
It's that kind of hubris, that bravado

leftover from a goddess who had me (in a myth we've lost),
that leads to me being carried by beak from the grass

to the concrete by a bird who's decided,
after smelling my cork

and sipping, that I taste
too young.

The bird, at Lucy's bidding (as a warning,
I hope, and not as a permanent state of things),

leaves me with all the moisture I've carried
as all the moisture I get,

fending for my desiccation-prone self
on a slab in a pyramid

made of sun.

Another attempt at a sun ode

Through a clearing in the tunnel of trees
on Warren Avenue: a view.

I become the one formerly walking. I forgive the view,

address the ode-worthy sun: *O sun like an old sun god retiring,
why do you insist that first thought's best thought,*

is God with a great big G?

And why do I listen in this awful heat
to a sun that begins its message

with, *To Whom it May Concern,* sending generic advice
for deciphering the cadence of *my* heart, which has climbed a hill,

is now at rest?

I wish the sun would begin with *Dear,* that it could do so without exploding,
that prior to dispensing advice

it would ask, *Is there an extra sandwich in your tote bag
that you'd be willing to share with me for lunch?*

I feel like ice enclosed by glass, like disemboweled light,
a bad marriage in a painting painted

when paintings had laws against divorce.

I ask the sun in the wispy voice of cloud, *Is it okay with you
that I've filled the plum of my mind with a boy*

*I call a sun-god seed? That all I do is done
to help him earn his freedom?*

I kick a small stone on his behalf.
I think of the boulder a glacier destroyed to make it.

O sun my sun, I've failed sincerely at bequeathing praise, am too consumed
tallying ways to be reduced, ways to make one think one has risen.

Like a lobbyist, I'm unable to advocate for anything other
than *this* station of my heart, dumb as a statistic,

thinking my mind's a place in which the praiser and praised both fit.

At the top of a hill, all bottoms in sight, I've reached the same end as the owl
I caught in a leg-hold trap, because the owl was hungry.

It tried to pluck a muskrat struggling in its own leg-hold trap,
tried to do so on an island in the middle of a quick-flowing stream
set with multiple traps,

which wasn't unwise based on the surface of things,
but for the owl was unfortunate due to things that lurked beneath.

It's the same demise reached by the man who never naps,
who finally succumbs to the urge on a hot summer day
when his work's done earlier than expected,

not anticipating that the body,
in retaliation for the napless years,

will counterbalance the dream of dreams he dreams when he finally sleeps
(on the old couch, on the porch, shoes on) by breathing so slowly

that he forgets this mother of dreams he remembers dreaming
in which he had it all, knew everything.

Hey, sun, did I ever tell you I make my own water in my mouth?
I do it routinely, and at will, and whenever I have a surplus

I spit, or think of spitting,
but hold it in because I can.

When you called to talk on New Year's Day

I turned down the volume on the Rose Bowl,
told you during the first lull in the conversation,

in order to fill the lull with seeds,

that the parakeet I heard singing just before you called
was trying to reach me

the way we try to reach intelligent life with our space probes.
The parakeet's song

was asking me to do whatever I could
to free things. I opened its cage door,

put newspapers in the middle of the floor
for it to shit on, thinking

Revolutions have begun like this. Have you ever looked
into the eye of a parakeet

for the secret of buoyancy, the secret of unencumbered flight?
Owning its song

on LP or CD would allow me to play it
loud enough to sing along,

loud enough to drown out
me trying to sing along (as if the song

were really mine, the singer me). I do that

with Bing Crosby and David Bowie
fusing "Little Drummer Boy" with "Peace on Earth,"

5 minutes and 48 seconds I think of as salvaged
from a black box at a crash site

where a UFO thought we wanted it to land,
everything at the accident scene

melted to a dot of gray
I have the power to reconstitute

by singing the song.

I have probably put too many seeds
in the lull, meaning nothing will grow.

You can't see it, but like a bird
whose ravenousness feeds

its rapidly beating heart, I am eating
these beans (seeds, peas, legumes)

foretold to bring nearly four hundred days of luck,
in case I only make it that long.

In this adventure of the rains, the runoff,

I wish I were speaking the language
predominant among those who conduct

multinational business

in the parallel universe where I'm not
counting eighteen carp in a shallow pool

that was part of the river when the river was wide
(I want to say wiser). I hover

above the carp like the gallery
at an experimental surgical procedure,

like a helicopter with no winch or rescue basket,
no divers on board.

The carp wait for a channel to be dredged,
are like ocean-liners in port

at the mercy of the captain of a tug. I crouch
close enough to pet one, worry that touching

a fish might feel to it
like burning. I leave the unresolved

unresolved, walk toward what we are wise to remember all

manner of river become:
twigs to their former trunk-like selves.

I lay belly to belly with the river's cold bank.

The grass is unrepentantly thankful for the water's receding.
I make a rough bed by crushing the grass.

I try to talk to a goose the river's coming and going has no mastery over.
I usher goose sound across the roof of my mouth,

make my tongue a reed, my palms a cave of air,
fingering my simple flute of a nose.

I convince the goose to swim toward me with a series of sounds
I can never repeat.

If you're trying to see it with your mind's eye,
as I will never not be able to see it in mine,

the dorsal fin on a carp emerged in water too shallow to submerge in,
bears no resemblance to the dorsal fin of a shark.

Picture instead a whale's oblong back
surfacing. Picture me

walking away, hoping the most bored, most runt,
most aquatically talentless of the dozen and a half carp

flops absurdly out of the pool
and slithers.

The other magicians will kill me for revealing all this

If you shave your head, you can see with the eyes
at the back of your head

unless GET YOUR FORTUNE TOLD signs
hang over the lids there.

It takes *one thousand one, one thousand two* . . . about five seconds
for two people passing

to realize they met in the chapter on bees.

She had a hand on her pepper spray, a hand on her phone.
A hand pulling on rope to tell the executioner to stop.

In jacket weather you carry in your pocket
lip balm, five of your favorite mouths,

candy you wish it were okay to give away to kids,
which it isn't, because of razor blades,

and apples, wackos
mixing the two,

which is why you feel hungover for drinking you didn't do,
it's the price of playing it cool.

The luxury of waiting for the light to change
hides (as luxuries do) the anxiety

the knees, as if bikini-clad and holding batons,
feel waiting for the signal to lead you

across the street. The brain after thinking
this about the knees

resolves that each of us is a pageant in storage.
It has time to send a memo to the feet and toes:

*The distance between you and the passing traffic
is the distance a medium-sized jungle cat can stretch.*

In case there are other brains
listening in,

yours passes a note, a crumpled ball you open
as carefully as you'd open a bud.

It says, *One kind of bleeding to death is from cuts
made to the body by pillows and sheets while you sleep.*

*Small "m" myth: only girls
are afraid to walk alone at night.*

The light's green. It's a whistle blown at a pitch
only you can hear.

What you can't hear it saying
is *go*.

Allegory of the beached

As if it were in, were the fashion,
neither you, nor I, nor any of our kind

lends a hand to the poor
jellyfish

who don't breathe or talk in
any sense of breathing

or talking we recognize. They don't have a role

in legend, aren't the porpoises and whales
we bend over backwards for, put along with the dead

we didn't honor enough during life
on stamps.

Brown being the new black, I've ordered
fried squid in sauce.

The menu announces its concern for my heart.
Swallowing, I'm a distraction

away from choking, from everyone
jumping up.

To dance as if coveter
and coveted

is Heimlich.

Making the beast with two backs.
I think but say. That but this.

Stamps no longer require the intimacy of a lick.

I, too, had a blue and gelatinous life.
I remember being happier then.

**A winter wind storm lead-pipes and cheap shots the wind chime,
like wind isn't a thing but things acting in the fashion of a mob,**

a gang that's decided beautiful random notes in a minor key
are something to be beaten up.

I hung the chime on a horizontal branch in spring,

on what looked like one of the tree's ears,
a lobe to dangle from. The tree conceived of

as one end of a teeter-totter,
me as fulcrum,

it's the Boeing 727s and whatnot overhead
that weigh the opposite end down.

A tree without easily discernible ears
probably doesn't contain the sensory capacity

to miss the wind chime.

A small old garage doing double duty as a shed
likely will not be in awe of the wind chime's potential
soundlessly hanging inside it.

Hoping that the tree might miss and the garage might
be in awe

is a disposition. I would never beat up anything

making beautiful random notes in a minor key.
One night I went to the Howard Johnson's bar

because we all thought that watching the antics of the divorced
picking up the divorced

would be a hoot. But the Howard Johnson's bar

isn't there anymore.
I can't go back to hug the divorcees with my eyes.

I hug that way more than I do with my hands
and arms.

I call it a disposition.

**A cold spell like this can keep you in the house
all gathered up like an oligarch**

All the chimneys spewing white, and all the white
threading together like braids,

as if our houses were the follicles hair grew from,
our neighborhood a head.

This message I'm receiving from the dead

is arriving un-signed, truncated,
both the picture and content abridged, like a decent movie

made unwatchable once it's edited
for TV. It's like

watching squirrels at work, calling it play,
them carrying in the teeth

whatever can be carried in the teeth,
the relics of our tiny hedonisms (potato skins, lime rinds)

like game pieces, squirrels
stippling patterns in the snow

on garage roofs, the patterns

easy enough to mistake for art. Easy enough to believe
that what we've put in the trash

is inspiration. That we and the squirrels

are on an assembly line
which cleverly doesn't look like one.

The squirrel that gets to the final square first
is so far ahead of the others

that there's nobody there to say, *you win*.

At eleven below zero a house shrinks into a fist.
I have two fists to pick from.

I would be a benevolent king, squirrel,
so select either one. No matter whether the watchers

tell the others it was on command
or demand, left or right (yours or mine),

something inside will warm you.

I can see the heart of the city now that the trees are nude

As seen through the exhalations of sewers, steamers, burners, breathers
is like glimpsing the ham bone in simmering soup,

then not. Is skyscrapers like plastic
replicas of skyscrapers glued to the lifelike grid of streets

in a snow globe. Is feeling sorry for the skyline,
how like a young celebrity

who doesn't want to be a role model for feminine virtue
anymore, it gives itself up from a distance,

from every direction
we can think to approach it.

The trees didn't drop their leaves in a striptease.
They pulled a curtain back.

It's like turning on the lights at a surprise party,
jumping up and spilling

your food or drink on somebody else.

The naked branches of trees
aren't scintillating at all

until you fathom that what they are
are cages torn apart from the inside out,

the unexplainable shivers and
brushes up against us by no one there:

free to do their thing.

And you thought I was dancing

I'm fighting on the Milky Way's side in the night-sky battle 'twixt it and
    the moon.

The trees that have lost their leaves are looking at each other
the way the longtime-bearded look in a mirror at a clean-shaven face,

muttering with accents that muddy-up the distinctions between d and t,
as would (wouldn't it?) be characteristic in high dung beetle.

And what if the remaining leaves itch? What if I could scratch them?
Very carefully. Maybe only rub them.

I want to found an old-fashioned nation-state
about which the encyclopedia says, *it's popular among the natives
to eat foods traditionally served at dinner*

for breakfast. I am hoping

to live long enough to see that every obvious correlation
I took for granted in my youth

matures into a causal relationship. Why say, *It's unseasonably warm,*
when you can say, *The weather itself is voting for its own ouster?*

Let's ask an entropy specialist
to quantify the energy in an exchange of pleasantries.

*Entropy specialist, Does "Hello" transfer more joules
than does an exchange of agreeable nods?*

We know that plus or minus two degrees Fahrenheit makes all the difference
in many worlds. You may ask

the feathery cloud to tell you about its days as ice,
as I just did.

Hello, economic slump. Hello, copper penny.

I'm trying to do the math but the math keeps changing.

Were I Jesus of the loaves and fishes, I would, with my one pot of coffee,
charge a whole lot of people up. I would ignore the math.

Hello, satellite,
showing us the former hurricane Iva
as it crawls up the Mississippi

like a fugitive who refuses to go to the hospital
to have the bullet removed.

As in a Hollywood ending, Iva will enter Minneapolis
as well-needed rain.

Pretty soon I, too, will be crawling and diminished with some kind of
    bullet in me.
Or so may go the conclusion of the rabbit
studying me from the bushes

as a rabbit anthropologist would.

Hello, meteorologists. If this is not your first life
I bet you were astrologers in a past one.

I just hit DELETE, acting as judge, jury, and executioner
(like Milgram said I would) to a line I was in love with.

You would've loved it, too. Now you'll have to pretend
you know exactly what I meant to say last.

Now they've put the spotlight
on both of us.

The brain before it's donated to science

It resists medication.

It remembers what it knows (and knows it knows)
about the imprisonment of naming.

It's glad for music, and also for everything harder to appreciate.
It's afraid that somebody trying to help

will accomplish the opposite
when they look inside and read back
a hackneyed rendition of the *there* there.

It imagines itself after body's death
when it becomes a self now outside of itself (outside of the formaldehyde jar)

as an old tube radio
being tuned, as knob and dial,

the first notes of a favorite song, reason

for another's nonstop
effort to clear the static away, fingers

tuning (left to right, right to left,
like foreplay). Once, it took for granted

signals sent to the throat,
the scream, the tongue,

fuel being transferred from the lungs.
It explains the circular saw

to the cicada, says, *Sorry about the impersonation,*
it's only a so-so performance, a too loud mimicry.

It speaks to where the cicadas are (in the trees
or the air between them), does so unselfconsciously

in front of a crow posed like it's the model for Crow,
model for the abyss,

old stand in for death and death-like shit.

**"it's not your normal eclipse," says
one blinded by it**

wanting
to do something
reciprocal
for the brilliant light
as thanks
for brilliance
for how it reminds one
to be thankful
for not-brilliance

for one's not-brilliance
remember
is another's
I ain't even got that much

and this wanting to do
doesn't get
no not anything
not
nothing
gets done

blame the sun.

•

one is he. one
is she. can be you. one
can be me. one
cannot do much
with a bad back.
one bad back

is just one bad back
actuarially. he
isn't much.
she's the world
to him. one
life to live in it
you get that
and bad backs
and odds stacked against you
and if you won't get off the couch
knowing that
dumb.

•

he named
the new fish
Memory. he didn't
feed it enough. then
he overfed it. Memory
went belly up, was flushed.
he couldn't remember
what Memory looked like
living. he closed his eyes
saw a kind of sun
on the dark side
of his lids.
he named the kind-of-sun
school of fish.
two hours later
he rethought his hasty decision
and renamed the sun
Marie.

•

in the rarest kind of eclipse
it's a stick figure, not a moon

that blocks the sun
is what he says

to her. she
holds a rock. sense

says she can't hold
her heart. he says

why not hold a seed
an egg, says

he's the stick figure. she says
she's not the sun.

she draws him then starts
a fire with her drawing of him.

he says the light is brilliant. she lets it

burn as out of control
as a drawing can.

III

Poem presented as an excuse for being so late

The raccoon I saw last night
was young, from this year's batch,
I could tell from the fact that it didn't fear me
as much as it ought to. At first I thought
it was a duck (dusk was up to its old tricks
with light. It may have thought I
were a leprous deer). When I said, *My friend
Steve Healey says more important things
more consistently than either Marx or Keynes*,
it didn't flee. *Long live St. Francis of Assisi*,
I said, and slept well enough, and have almost
returned full circle to where the story
began, a suburban pond
across a walk bridge from a suburban marsh
(perhaps connected, one feeding another)
where one can pause to be heady as this,
and from where I fear
the raccoon I courted last night
is the one I just passed, flattened,
we say, but it was more like rolling hills
of viscera and fur. Dead in the road.
As St. Francis occurred then, Nietzsche and Sartre
do now. I've been reading about
quantum mechanics and want to discuss
string and bounce and black-hole-as-
door theory. I want to tell the raccoon
that I slept on it and I'm pretty
sure I'd have the gumption
to chew off my leg if it were caught
in a trap. I set my cup on the rail. It starts to spin
slowly around. There's no such thing as ghosts
is what I'm hoping I've discovered
the equal and irrefutable opposite of. My eye, it turns out,

is fixated on a tiny red spider, size of a black pepper flake,
circumnavigating my coffee cup's rim. The spinning
is only a kind of spinning, different from
but a lot like spinning in place.

It's October, and a lot of things, including the usual carpetbaggers, summer, and the leaves on trees, are gone or going

The bark-boring insects
that took out all of the trees on our street, a true truth of my childhood,

becomes a way to understand what's happening now,
gravity's plus or minus thirty-two feet per second squared

making arrangements to bury its father *(Newton
didn't really feel the thud of an apple on his head).*

New truth, smaller than a bread box, used in a sentence:
Lincoln didn't love the slaves as much as we'd like to think.

I say to the buds I can't see,
speaking less to trees, more to a belief in spring, to unborn flora,

*The footings set when you were not yet a high-rise you,
in the bedrock of your formative years, in the low,*

low layers underneath your growth above it: what happens is

*the footings, like anything else after long enough,
start to give way (a pronouncement, note takers,
from which "giving way" is spared).*

The frizzy-haired lady, who looks like the lady on the jacket of a book
on my shelf, walking her little dog

on the sidewalk that moats our homes,
hears me say, *Go, go, go!*

as encouragement to the buds. She says
go, too, like the embodiment

of an echo with conspiratorial intent. It feels as if the frizzy-haired lady
and I are side by side, on massage tables, being kneaded

as the President's Chef would knead the President's Dough.
As if we're conspiring in the place of dying

to drop ourselves off like luggage
that holds who we are, have been, and may (more conspiracy)

get lucky enough to be. Us
as bags the host dreads offering to take care of

after seeing how many there are, *but upon picking one up
and finding it light*

*day-dreams is filled with crepes,
or toast or parsley, or maybe half-filled, the rest—*

says the frizzy-haired lady—*bouquet.*

**I forgot my umbrella and am starting to see things newly now,
as if with seldom-used eyes at the back of my head**

Cold raindrops are hammer blows.
Summer is the wall coming down.

As if there's a work ticket.

As when metal hits metal, as with the quick
birth and death of sparks,

there should be *oooing* and *ahhing*.

The city geese brothel on the spring-fed ponds

and on the ponds by the power plant
that never freeze.

They don't care that the rain will turn to snow
once the demo's complete.

Whomever painted the sparrows painted the bark that hides them
with the same brush and can.

The sparrows are as brave as soldiers in a Great War ode,
demanding the rights to migration

from the geese. Stamina, more wingspan, larger hearts and lungs,
the migrator's internal GPS

are what we'll all march in the streets for next.

I like seeing resilience in a cold, cold rain.
Yesterday I had an umbrella. All I saw was a shitty day.

You can't take it back after you click SEND

Had I known, early on I would have pulled and composted the kale
I planted in the window box

that for $2.49 was supposed to flower.
Holding and turning it, I feel like a depiction

above a caption that says, *Had I known early on,*
I wouldn't have allowed the shame of underachievement

to age the kale as rapidly
as presidents. Kale the color of sand. Threadbare.

As if the kale-moths
had eaten holes. As if the kale were auditioning

to be the costume worn by the ghost of Christmas past, present, or future,
whichever is worse off

in the eye of the moviemaker.

The rest of the outdoors
swells out green chest after green chest,

like a stadium of fans.

Had I composted the kale, it would have been well on its way
to being loam by now, worth less pound for pound

than when its tag promised it would flower, but
on the side of the living.

Had I known, I wouldn't have sent the e-mail
in which I disparaged my kale.

I wouldn't have given away that piece of my mind.

I would've written all my thoughts down, would've slept on them,
and in the morning (in the only surviving illustration)

would've selected the entire passage.
I would've started to type again,

plagiarizing from the way the tulip stems stand there,
say nothing I'll remember an hour from now, end up better off for it,

if tomorrow is a fair measure, if the life cycle of a tulip
can save me, this is how.

The brain in the body in the house whose owner you curse, call a lazy piece of shit

It reads some Proust
while quieting the stomach
with what billboards
along the esophagus say
is a cousin of the oatmeal
Gallway eats alone,
is lumpish and willing
to disintegrate, is incantatory.
The brain would prefer
Proust's *epidermis of light*
to the suit it wears out
wearing, saying things like
Out of the nowhere
the brain knows is
really a somewhere unnamed:
the memory of a newspaper
and a bloody mary and
hashed-browns—a still life
featuring the suit when
it was newer, a me as
the better of me trying
to best myself again
by calling the black cat
using a boot for a pillow
Marcel, the brown cat
on the sill *Kinnell*, which
feels like prelude to playing
dress-up, which prompts
a groin that has never
been tied to a bed (it says)
to prepare for it. In this
transcript of eating breakfast

alone slowly as a way
to delay the clearing
of last night's snow from
the walk, which has to be
done to avoid a ticket,
the brain stops thinking
about the shovel and allows
the arms and hands that
have written checks
for fines to wield it.
After the snow's cleared,
is what the brain promises
the stomach and its child's
attention span, *you
will have earned
a sandwich made with
leftover turkey (with
after-life)*, a voice
in the bowels out of
the nowhere says
on record must be eaten
today or thrown.

Old me would go from holding-up to leading, would put the transmission into gear and drive

It can be a morning like any other.

Hard to tell when geese will decide to walk

across the road instead of fly.

What the sun can do with moles and hairs and veins:

I look for a nose, ears, eyes, lips,

cheeks and a chin, a facsimile

of Jesus's, or Anne Sexton's, or John Belushi's,

or young Muhammad Ali's face.

The driver behind me honks.

The rearview shows I'm holding-up

a line of cars. I tune the radio

to LOVE 105. I want to see us

from a vantage point where we resemble

a marching band. The geese will

wake tomorrow with sore knees.

The geese were/ are gone

in the style of *poof*.

New me can't get over

how my engine sounds so

goddamn happy idling.

Poem like the stock in which the Thanksgiving turkey lasts all winter, assuaging in a way that time never will by pretending to make time stand still

A gray squirrel with a red squirrel's tail,
grown like the wrong answer
from its haunches and spine,
is just a gray squirrel
with a red squirrel's tail, a minor stewing
executed in the blameless womb
after squirrel-on-squirrel love
in the area shaded yellow
and shaped like a tube sock
on at least one map
where the ranges of the two
kinds of squirrels overlap.
Growing zone 4a. Where you can harvest
some of the best Yellow Globe onions
you've ever seen, and can also
get a Yellow Globe
that isn't as sweet
as it should be for all
the careful hybridization.
Is more oblong than round. The yellow
sickly, like its got a bad liver,
is only a sketch, something
only we do-nothing sitters at windows
ever notice. Stautue-ishly perched.
Buddha-ishly hoping
we'll be born a next time
as the condensation that collects
on windows when soup
is simmered on a cold,
cold night. That we'll become
the colors of the kitchen,

the colors of all the outdoor lights.
That all sides constituting
the other side be seen
through us, blurred by we
who will evaporate while you sleep.
Who will be gone in the morning.
And won't have left a note.

A public slide where the gleaming steel has been shinned just about frictionless by asses in blue jeans and also in fancier clothes

After fire and tools, representative democracy,
the blurring of high and low culture,

there were wars, assassinations,
some great films,

factories making passwords on demand.

We'd become minor gods put into our places by major ones,
in factory jobs, handed planet after planet to fill.

Around the time psychology was becoming as precise as physics,
we had, each of us,

as many passwords as school janitors used to have keys on a ring
in the era before keyless locks, maybe more.

One Tuesday when the Cubs were winning, lost in happiness,
for the Cubs were winning, somebody forgot what comes after 007

at the ATM, couldn't get what he'd gone to the store for.
He'd gone for salmon.

It struck him as fitting that salmon are dying out.

He sat and got ready to pick up crazy-speed.
He is not a euphemism for me.

I'm on the ladder watching
how they throw up their arms for dramatic effect,

how life takes place on metal stairs, left leg leading the right, or just about the same is right leading the left.

We the people provide our own propulsion.

Those determined to milk it develop a signature scream,
learn how to wave their fingers like they're electrocuted fish.

That drop-gut feeling that feels like the stomach rising up behind the lungs
is an illusion, but is no less exhilarating

than the stomach rising up and out of your mouth for real.

Another attempt at an ode to the cardinal

After sunset it sings how sunset would sing if sunset had a syrinx,
if it could control points along its own trachea independently.

But sunset can't do that, and because it can't—because it's like a child blind since birth,

whose overly compensatory sense of hearing is as keen as a deer's—
sunset plays the bird's throat

with fingers you wouldn't believe
are made only of refracted light,

like the cardinal is hopped-up, is electric,
is backfeed-infused.

I almost say *play it again*, almost call the sunset Sam.
But before I can do that

darkness—always darkness—grows over the song, the uneventful day,
a beard over the seeable,

until I can't tell the difference between the bird's red feathers and tree's green leaves.
To pass the time while my eyes grow accustomed, which may take until morning,

tell me what day was ever uneventful? Is there any such thing as radio silence?
Tomorrow, will you sing or listen best?

**There's soup in the dome of my ladle
too deep to lick out, my tongue not the tongue of an anteater,**

my ladle designed by utensil-makers with architectural blood
dreaming of the Taj Mahal.

I wash it out, add ladle detritus to the list of gifts given to sewers
and lakes via drains.

I'm sad for the failings of my modest tongue,
which is scarred from getting caught once in the middle of biting down.

That my ladle, under a spell or charged by lightning,
could become a living thing

is something I don't tell my tongue.

Try counting all the ladles made of rock and bone,
all the canyons, skulls, and sockets.

My grandmother's soup contained wind, light,
and anti-light,

fear of accusations of insanity.

I have washed the food from dishes sufficient to have saved
so many starving lives.

Thinking and cooking and cleaning, I've watched four dogs grow old
and die. I am only beginning to understand

why my mother's mother didn't write her recipes down,

why the tongue I taste the soup with
returns each morning

having sung its songs tree to tree, city to city,
reeking of whale and brine.

This is the brain wishing Dr. Frankenstein had perfected his procedure, that one of his protégé could transplant it into a body made of younger parts

The wish is a flower grown from a seed dropped here.
The seed was a flier tacked to an electrical pole, a photo and the words "Lost Dog."

At the time the brain was helping the heart cope.
The heart was losing a love, so the flier didn't help.

The brain raised the hands and closed the eyes and explored the rough skin of a stuccoed wall.

It was mimicking the actress preparing for a role in which she's eyeless.

The brain was telling the heart that things could be worse.
This nurtured the seed, and although the dog on the flier was mature,

the brain, with a little misdirection, like a pump fake,
took to imagining a puppy born in summer,

who, if it survives ownerlessness, will, as a stray,
invent God

when the tree it pees beneath in the park
sheds its leaves.

Brain to heart: I've been speaking to some senior citizens I'm close to and can report that *within the normal range*

is a cave you hide inside
when the matter is a count of the cells

that fight cancer (and the behaviorally—but let's hold off on a diagnosis—
but, yes, cancer-like). A stem grows, and leaves.

One day the brain makes motivational pleas,
says we all should try to be more like the sparrows who delight in a
   bath in the alley
where the trash receptacles are lined up for pick up,

the sparrows ecstatic because so late in the year
the dirty water that collects in the potholes between 40th and 41st

isn't frozen. That the knees ache vaguely
is the brain's acknowledgment

that if you're beautiful and are chewing with your mouth open wide
you not only won't offend, but will seduce.

Pushing a bud through takes a toll on the stem
is all I'm saying,

and after the flowering the tired stem's
got no place to go.

There's this crow in my neighborhood without a tail, an aeronautic mess
that has taught itself to fly, to takeoff and land without a rudder,
so against the odds and yet so in control,

it's the one crow the smaller birds
don't gang up to chase or mock.

It's a crow the stem idolizes, and makes it not mind
how the gild of the golden years rubs off

because we always touch them too much.

There is morning and there are passages from dreams, seven-minute spans
that seem to last longer than that, when the brain speaks as the I,

promises to keep on wishing its wishes for wishing's sake,
doing so as an offering to the god whose name it would have to look up,
whose secondary or tertiary duty is governing the passage of time in bed

when you're not sure whether it's *you* you, or the one in the dream,
or the one there beside *you* you

who's in control of the hands
touching what you've learned to call yourself.

Where I-494 delineates suburban Bloomington from suburban Richfield

Driving is driving plus plus when it's driving like a fish
in water, which is what driving's like beneath a winter sky
that looks like a body of water's surface
as seen from below—it looks like a scarf of clouds,
rumpled and creased, made of elephant's skin
but without the elephant hairs, skin
as seen in close-ups of elephants taken by Nikons
pointed and operated by people who know that selling the shot
will earn them enough to buy a grilled cheese,
but a grilled cheese only gets you so far,
so they take more close-ups, shoot landscapes
equivalent to three squares a day, 365 days a year, year in and
out as the great fortune of being able to do what you love
becomes doing what you love for money, and the market
has a say in that, and with markets pointing and clicking
at you, you can't help but feel prostituted, which is worse
than whoring yourself out—I say that knowing both—
and really I wouldn't mind being a whore for the sky,
opening all the way up to these clouds moving
north en masse. March of the deliberate. Sky as river.
Clouds as ice. If I block out traffic in the lanes left and right,
use my visors like the blinders on a horse, put my face
for a dangerously long time to the windshield, if I say
abracadabra, alakazam, maybe I'll feel like a horse, not driving
but driven, prodded by a rider beneath whom I'm toiling,
only I can't envision who my rider might be, but
I'm carrying a rider's weight in my back, and I don't know
why I thought being a horse would be better than
being me. I still haven't crashed. Instead of a horse
I've become an insect flying over elephant terrain,
coming in for a landing on an elephant's ear, which means
elephants and the bugs that pester them

have everything to do with the winter sky announcing
that one mitten will be lost for every four pulled on, everything to do
with minor crashes, with their thousands of dollars
in damage, all this Africa infusing, which isn't taxable, nobody
will pay you to be that fly, if that's what the insect I am is,
if there are flies as green as emeralds who don't have agents
to sign release forms and negotiate royalties for the photos
free lancers take of them, flies as unrepresented
as the ones we shoo from the uncovered food we eat
when we eat outside in summer. I nearly crashed
a second ago. I imagined what ascending
to the heavens would be like, burning the clouds
like I'm pizza, like I'm hot hot hot, like the clouds
are the roof of God's mouth, and I am a kind of victory.

The serendipity of good light for taking photos in

is like a high-interest line of credit
to be withdrawn from

at times when I know I can't but wish I could
change the face on me to reflect a change within.

Photo: I thought I looked pretty smart
in my white pants, but should've remembered
as I thought,

I look pretty smart in these white pants,
to indulge in the long tradition

of sacrificial offerings
to goddesses who can move from the sky

into our bodies, living out as much of the rest of our lives
as they please there.

I had yet to learn the phrase *gang aft agley*, so when things went,
as they say, from perpetually dry to perpetually damp

I said, *fuck fuck fuck fuck fuck fuck fuck fuck motherfuck shit*.

The vow never to wear white pants again
is part of my collection

of canary-in-the-mineshaft-y corpses,

the valiant lives of which I record
on opposite but facing pages

in a book remarkably heavy for its size.

Photo: I am eating the far-fetched soup for lunch.

Journal entry: All day long I talked about
my bad lunch. No one who heard me

will ever go to the place where I got the crappy far-fetchedness
ever again. It is as if I have dropped a stone

into the still pond, in the gravity-free and frictionless world
where ponds exist because a word for them does.

Tidal waves blossom from the dropped stone.
There's no unblossoming.

Another way to drop a stone is to collapse into a ball,
like an ottoman

somebody else can rest their feet on.

From another page in the notebook: My stance is opposite
the stance of wind, sun, snow, rain, and hail,

which take matter-of-factly
the small or large tragedy that caused

the "event cancelled" notice,
fading the eight-by-eleven-inch sheet

of 24-pound goldenrod
to bones of the long dead collected in a gully

white. Photo: I fold the notice into a boat,
draw in cargo, passengers, crew,

who only drawn can send
no discernible SOS

as the boat takes on the runoff from winter
in the lowland next to the curb

where (journal entry with my white pants secretly on)
a harrowing movie

all about the dangers of rivers
plays with a kind of dizzying IMAX effect

that makes you duck and scream
and grab the person next to you,

as if you're falling from the sky, wantonly believing
you can't die with a goddess inside.

Half of the battle of learning is learning what it is you can write for yourself

One thing I can write for myself is the book of pulling on socks,
book of tying laces so my ankles are harnessed in the manner of oxen

that pull the heart, the stomach,
takes them on strolls.

The other half of the battle of learning, whether you're learning on ice
or on the stickier oval of a roller rink,

is accepting that there are things
that have to be written for you.

If you can skate forward only, you'll never forget the girls
you would've loved to hold hands with

but who would only skate with those who could skate in reverse.

Time, fab teacher of we lesser storytellers, with its penchant for seizing
   a heart,
using a farmer's own grain against him

to smother him in a bin, throws a girl into the air, into an *up there*
from which she might never return.

Breath-holding while we wait for her to
feels like a test run at killing oneself.

Time stands naked
before the full-length mirror in its hotel room, wondering

if a medal against its chest would be cold.

Just as naked on the other side of the wall,
in an adjoining room with the door locked,

I'm writing the story of the goose that fell asleep dreaming
of its thin-air high,

woke with its feet frozen in ice, like it was a kind of handle
on a kind of lid covering the lake,

which is the story of the prospect of pressure building
until it becomes the story of flight.

If you hit your man harder than he hits he you, he's the one who'll hurt more works for football, not for collisions with the sun

Crow collides with sun more violently than I do
when I'm standing beneath a leafed or leafless

this tree or that. It's blackness

absorbs the blow. When I think it's like a mother
humming a child to sleep,

crow stirs, shows me it has no trousers, doesn't carry cash.
Radios are tuned to favorite stations nobody agrees on.

In our make-believe Mexico City, neither crow nor I can find the consulate,
or a public toilet,

or a free taco happy hour.

I leave the backyard to escape the buzz of circular saws,
walk into the buzz of cicadas in the front.

The silent middle place

where one can tuck a head under a wing,
pull a pillow under, sleep:

I walked by so quickly I missed it. I was preoccupied
trying to fit a moistened wad of loose leaf

into the gutted core of an ink pen.

I thought I heard crying for help.
I wanted to arrive in the dramatic, in the hair-raising,

in some well-told story's nick of time. I want, I confess,

somebody to screw a plaque into a rock
saying how hard we've tried.

**The question the Farmer's Almanac answers about winter
is whether it will be mild or harsh, but the question I have isn't that**

Over the years, across the species, the constant among the winter wishes
is to be small and sheltered and inside of something.

A hand out of pocket. You in the cold.

The old wish for fire and a cave and bear grease,
warm bodies and heated stones

to huddle with under fur
has evolved

into the wish that your ride would arrive soon. Think

squirrel is to tree hollow as bear is to den
as you are to the chocolate center of a Tootsie Pop,

sheltered by hard candy
it takes an as-yet-unknown number of licks to break through. Weird

that we know how much an atom of iodine weighs.
Weirder that the people of the future, wishing they were sheltered and small,

will look back and think we were dumb.

Ruminations on the cud from seven of my fullest stomachs

My brothers who are not my brothers,
who are my sisters, who like wildflowers
from season to season depend on wind, I'm
sorry it's Saturday, that none of us have access
to the parts or schematics we need
to fix all the broken-downs
we've left scattered about. (*We found them inside us,
were born this way*,
we are tempted to say.) Feel
free to overgrow them, to refer to us
as glaciers that passed through
ages ago. My brothers who are not my brothers,
who are my sisters but were once
of the same nothingness, thanks
for your blooming, for your lips, for the springtime
buds Lucille calls *these hips*.

•

While tangents may intersect
points too small to measure, they're
everywhere and in the aggregate
weigh way more than you think
something so close to zero could.
You can swap them like baseball cards
and get to know one another
very well.

•

In a dream a crow and I shared last night,
like a blind date, I was cast as Clarence the Angel,
the crow was George Bailey. If you bought

tickets to the dream I'm sorry
I can't refund whatever it was you paid,
the ending was awfully French, or maybe
it was 1970s American based on the French. Maybe
the crow got his wings and maybe he didn't.
It's hard to tell. Maybe the crow was a girl.
Maybe Bedford Falls is more pot than park
no matter who runs the bank. Maybe in heaven
angels work the night shift on the line
just like they do in Sioux City.

•

When next you see steam
rise from that which, or who, seems to be sleeping, examine
yourself by asking if your focus is on the steam
or on the sleeper, like you're a story problem
in mid-solve and are solving yourself
and have to select an oval to fill in
before A) we, B) were, C) we're,
or D) I.

•

Standing still and almost not-breathing,
you long for that catch-your-breath breathing
the body indulges in after flight. You wish
a dog would give you reason—
you'd call it *the courage*—to scatter.

•

There's the dumb but catchy song
that won't leave my head, and the wishing
a sort of fist were winding up

in my belly, getting ready to throw a blow along the spinal column,
punching the song out through my nose, like a hefty sneeze.
Not appreciating the song
as somebody's *It's our song!*
and feeling bad about it
allows "The Way We Were"
to replace it, like an avalanche moving through things
not meant to be moved through,
killing everybody who came to ski
down what had seemed to be permanence,
what had presented itself
as immovability.

•

A: You'll grind your coffee beans way too fine
if you engage your memory
when what you should be using
are mainly your hands and eyes
Q: How did we get to this acrid taste?

It's on the way back that walking there starts to seem like a bad idea

He opens his mouth to help him envision
an O-ring. He says, *This is space-shuttle bad.*

Fire frozen to water. Something like dry ice.
Something sinisterly comic's

insinuation of the bottom-of-the-glass part
of Dante's hell.

An invitation for the soul
to step out of costume

is a way to think of it, the snow one falls asleep in,
the atmosphere at 43,000 feet

(which he remembers it takes
73 seconds to reach).

This many blocks from home, without a cover for his face,
he looks up,

as if at the first eclipse, watches
This is space-shuttle bad

dissipate at 20 feet. Anything would.
He remembers being taught

by a holy man
who in his old age was found out also to be a sodomizing man—

from whom he learned nothing
about blow jobs

(*Did he find me ugly?* dissipates).

He learned that you can baptize a baby
in an emergency, in the back of a cab,

or in the desert, or on horseback,
with nothing more than spit.

There but for

Sprinting across the roof of the porch,
a squirrel that's never seen a horse.

If it were a country squirrel, mountain squirrel,
rodeo, circus, or cartoon squirrel, not a center of the city squirrel,

it might hear its own sprinting
and brush out on the easel of *hell yeah*

itself galloping like a horse with wings,

which would put us in competition with each other,
building to takeoff speed.

The squirrel leaps safely from house to tree.

It's not that I haven't dreamed of spontaneously combusting into a bird,
but when my scapula itches

I scratch it, use my fingernails like farm implements,
plowing furrows into my skin,

taming the bird portion (today's whimsy) of the half-bird/half-man
I perhaps was meant to be.

Must suck to be born a squirrel that's never seen paintings of angels.

Must suck to be a church squirrel that's never seen comic book creatures
putting the angels to shame.

Six cups of coffee is one way to build up speed.

Once I saved another
from something like the open fields of carefree youth

by pushing the other into something like the safety of a trench.
I hoped (whimsy of ago) a not quite lethal dose of the youth I saved the
   other from

would transfer to, and reinvigorate me (I hoped I could jump
all the way to Asia Minor

if that's where I wanted to be). I can say, *Flame on*,
and do. Sinatra is singing *come fly with me*.

Now my other scapula itches. Now my thighs. My face.
Maybe *scratch where it itches* is a leash.

Maybe I'll have my fingernails removed.

**In addition to watching a football game
none of our teams are playing in**

We dream up a parts house
we've never been to

where the carburetors are less machine

than they are pink and alive, like hearts
plucked from a body at a wreck, packed in ice,

kept in the kinds of coolers we buy off shelves,
use on any other day to keep our beer cold.

We open the lid to the cooler that does that—keeps our beer cold—
watch a 3D-miniaturist's version of a foggy morning

rise like the air above a lake
on a chilly day in fall,

like the idea of a white bird exactly as it occurred to the god of evolving things
before it was shaped and named and ornithologized

as pelican, snow goose, swan.

We drink away what we know of fog being distinguished from mist
and of mist and fog being prelude to bird

based on the density of each.

We swear that the chicken preceded the egg.
We swear vice versa. Swear

(our country knows quakes)

that the bedrock beneath the cooler
shifted overnight, and the spring that feeds it,

while we slept, was ravished by flame.

This is the brain feeling slighted, and so adopting mechanisms pursuant to its defense

Finding in the morning an inch of snow when ten were predicted
to fall overnight, a ten the brain expected

to cancel or postpone the routines and obligations
that thicken it, ten

reporting for duty as one, so you can't just grab a shovel

and lose yourself making a path
with high white walls through drifts

becoming whiteness itself,
becoming the cold,

which is why the prediction of deep snow
feels like a promise broken.

To compensate, the brain charts a map of North America
upon which the migratory flyways are lit up

like we light up O'Hare, which is the brain playing God,
flying to a south it harbors within, hearing echoes

of itself thinking *God*, thinking *Oz*,

the words barreling like walls of water
down the crevasses of its own gray matter.

The brain is sorry there isn't a disclaimer, something

to say that the thinking today is brought to you by woe,
by the brian playing dead

as if it were caught in a crowd
being sprayed with automatic weapons, or were a possum

a kid's beating with his dad's seven iron,

so now the brain is seeking forgiveness for arms, for youth,
for automatic weapons,

and it seeks it in an inch of snow
which was supposed to be ten inches of snow, loving it

like it's learned to love most things, which isn't less,
but differently, or is maybe differently

and a little less, or differently instead of less, which neither brain
nor body will discuss.

Stretching for a run to work off more than just the take-out you've been eating so much of,

because it might be true, what the empiricists and personal trainers say, that mind and body are one,

and it's the body's turn to sweat profusely,

stretching as if you were embryo
of the run itself,

which might take place on a treadmill,
or around a cinder track, or in a park

where you Napoleon the demarcations
push the baby, score the points.

May you once in your tenure run along the sidewalks of a city thinking,
What mollusks we ships of happenstance host!

The cosmos are too big
for the slow bat speed of the human mind

occurs to you like you're a notebook

collecting scraps you will later assemble
into pages of your soft-speaking chapter (we all get one)

in *The Collected Works of Bugs*

Mummified in Webs That Will No Longer Have Tensile Relevance
After One Comes Though With a Broom.

There is the miracle of running in place
while not running at all, listening like one

about to convert
to your ridiculed ostrich innerness, which is telling you

to run as fast as you can and when your legs feel like stone,
run out of them.

What we know about physics is proof (inner ostrich says)
that a fast enough runner running counter to the rotation of the earth

can bring the earth to a halt.

What we know about airplanes
says he, she, or it, running that fast, can put the arms out,

tilt the hands just so, and fly away.

Acknowledgments

Versions of the following poems have appeared in the following journals, sometimes with a different title:

Connotation Press: "Where I-494 delineates suburban Bloomington from suburban Richfield," "The question the Farmer's Almanac answers about winter is whether it will be mild or harsh, but the question I have isn't that"

Blood Lotus: "For every obvious thing, there's a three-dimensional chess set of subtextual things," "'May you live through a thousand winters,' like 'aloha,' is our greeting" (reprinted in the Blood Lotus 10-year anthology), "The other magicians will kill me for revealing all this"

Spinning Jenny: "You say 'promise,'" "Poem like an old thumb-on-the-spool baitcasting reel, meant to attach to a rod and practice with in the park, rather than hang useless on nails in your garage, so that if or when you get a magic lamp the practice pays off, and what you don't do is freeze, losing your one shot with a genie emerged"

South Dakota Review: "Allegory of the beached"

ILK: "Another attempt at a sun ode"

Revolver: "May they all, your dreams, come true in the end," "In order that I shall last as long as I can," "In addition to watching a football game none of our teams are playing in," "This is the brain feeling slighted, and so adopting mechanisms pursuant to its defense," "Stretching for a therapeutic run to work off more than just the take-out you've been eating so much of," "The clog I can't get unclogged which I'll probably never tell you about (the drinking on company time I will)"

The Chariton Review: "She loves me, she loves me not," "Thoughts like the molecules of exhaust that graduate to visibly as they exit a tailpipe, tho' never last long enough to shape themselves into rhinos or yachts or friendly ghosts (as clouds do), serving only to remind you it's cold," "In this adventure of the rains, the runoff"

Paper Darts: "The true story of how I learned that the graveyard shift meets at Prince's for drinks at 6:30 a.m."

The Rumpus: "Ruminations on cud from seven of my fullest stomachs"

So and So Magazine: "People being mostly water and not nocturnal"

I Thought I Was New Here: "What you won't see here is Orion, for it's neither winter nor night (a Uruguayan, you couldn't see the Southern Cross)," "A winter wind storm lead-pipes and cheap shots the wind chime, like wind isn't a thing but things acting in the fashion of a mob," "The brain in the body in the house whose owner you curse, call a lazy piece of shit"

Barn Owl Review: "Like a matryoshka doll separated from the set during some long-ago scttling of affairs"

Sugar House Review: "This is the brain stuck on a line from a movie," "Another attempt at an ode to the cardinal"

Descant: "When will it be too late to apply lessons learned?," "This is the brain wishing Dr. Frankenstein had perfected his procedure, that one of his progeny could transplant it into a body made of younger parts," "Half of the battle of learning is learning what it is you can write for yourself"

Water~Stone Review: "it's not your normal eclipse, says one blinded by it"

Editor to editor, thanks to the staffs of the journals who published poems appearing in this manuscript, and also to the staffs of journals who carefully read and respectfully rejected them. Thanks, too, to those who've hosted the readings where I've tested these poems in public. Thanks to the Poetry City, USA crew, comrades-in-poetry-arms, and to everybody who does their part to make the Twin

Cities a reader's and writer's Shangri-La. Thanks to my poet and writer friends. What you all do (all of the aforementioned) makes the big engine go. Thanks to everybody who makes THP a poetry family you want to come home to. Thanks to Sara Lefsyk and Paula Cisewski for helping to turn the manuscript into this book. Thanks especially to Tayve Neese for her editorial guidance and shaping, and to Sara Lefsyk (again) and Dorinda Wegener for conjuring amazing design from the words on the page. Thanks to all three of them for friendship after the work's done. I miss and thank Wednesday and Zooey, great cats who sat with me as I wrote and read these poems aloud, the former having lived a good, long life, the latter dying way too soon (Cleo and Charlie have taken their batons and will get their due on any books that follow). Thanks to my not-poet friends and family for many things, but particularly, in this context, for being proud and supporting what they don't quite get. Thanks to Angie for accommodating me-as-poet, and for everything, everything else.

About the Author

Matt Mauch is the author of *If You're Lucky Is a Theory of Mine* (Trio House Press, 2013), *Prayer Book*, and the chapbook *The Brilliance of the Sparrow*. His poems have appeared in numerous journals, including *Conduit, DIAGRAM, Willow Springs, The Los Angeles Review, Forklift, Ohio, Sonora Review, H_NGM_N, Water~Stone Review, The Mississippi Review*, and on the *Poetry Daily* and *Verse Daily* websites. Mauch edits *Poetry City, USA*, a journal of poetry and prose on poetry, and lives in Minneapolis, where he teaches in the AFA in Creative Writing program at Normandale Community College.

About the Artist

Sara Lefsyk lives in Colorado where she bakes, writes and makes various mixed-media art pieces.

About the Book

Bird~Brain was designed at Trio House Press through the collaboration of:

Tayve Neese, Lead Editor
Sara Lefsyk, Supporting Editor
Sara Lefsyk, Cover Art
Dorinda Wegener, Cover Design
Lea Deschenes, Interior Design

The text is set in Adobe Caslon Pro.

The publication of this book is made possible, whole or in part,
by the generous support of the following individuals and/or agencies:

Anonymous

About the Press

Trio House Press is a collective press. Individuals within our organization come together and are motivated by the primary shared goal of publishing distinct American voices in poetry. All THP published poets must agree to serve as Collective Members of the Trio House Press for twenty-four months after publication in order to assist with the press and bring more Trio books into print. Award winners and published poets must serve on one of four committees: Production and Design, Distribution and Sales, Educational Development, or Fundraising and Marketing. Our Collective Members reside in cities from New York to San Francisco.

Trio House Press adheres to and supports all ethical standards and guidelines outlined by the CLMP.

Trio House Press, Inc. is dedicated to the promotion of poetry as literary art, which enhances the human experience and its culture. We contribute in an innovative and distinct way to American Poetry by publishing emerging and established poets, providing educational materials, and fostering the artistic process of writing poetry. For further information, or to consider making a donation to Trio House Press, please visit us online at: www.triohousepress.org.

Other Trio House Press Books you might enjoy:

Break the Habit by Tara Betts, 2016

Bone Music by Stephen Cramer
    2015 Louise Bogan Award selected by Kimiko Hahn

Rigging a Chevy into a Time Machine and Other Ways to Escape a Plague by Carolyn Hembree
    2015 Trio Award Winner selected by Neil Shepard

Magpies in the Valley of Oleanders by Kyle McCord, 2015

Your Immaculate Heart by Annmarie O'Connell, 2015

The Alchemy of My Mortal Form by Sandy Longhorn
    2014 Louise Bogan Winner selected by Carol Frost

What the Night Numbered by Bradford Tice
    2014 Trio Award Winner selected by Peter Campion

Flight of August by Lawrence Eby
    2013 Louise Bogan Winner selected by Joan Houlihan

The Consolations by John W. Evans
    2013 Trio Award Winner selected by Mihaela Moscaliuc

Fellow Odd Fellow by Steven Riel, 2013

Clay by David Groff
    2012 Louise Bogan Winner selected by Michael Waters

Gold Passage by Iris Jamahl Dunkle
    2012 Trio Award Winner selected by Ross Gay

If You're Lucky Is a Theory of Mine by Matt Mauch, 2012

www.ingramcontent.com/pod-product-compliance
Lightning Source LLC
Chambersburg PA
CBHW020618300426
44113CB00007B/690